Date Due

WRITE YOUR OWN

ADVENTURE

STORY

by Tish Farrell

First published in the United States in 2006 by
Compass Point Books
3109 West 50th Street #115
Minneapolis, MN 55410

Copyright © ticktock Entertainment Ltd 2006
First published in Great Britain in 2006 by ticktock Media Ltd.,
ISBN 1 86007 532 0 PB
A CIP catalogue record for this book is available from the British Library.

Visit Compass Point Books on the Internet at
www.compasspointbooks.com
or e-mail your request to
custserv@compasspointbooks.com

For Compass Point Books
Sue Vander Hook, Nick Healy, Anthony Wacholtz, Nathan Gassman, James Mackey,
Abbey Fitzgerald, Catherine Neitge, Keith Griffin, and Carol Jones

For ticktock Entertainment Ltd
Graham Rich, Elaine Wilkinson, John Lingham,
Suzy Kelly, Heather Scott, Jeremy Smith

Library of Congress Cataloging-in-Publication Data
Farrell, Tish.
    Write your own adventure story / by Tish Farrell.
        p. cm.—(Write your own)
    Includes bibliographical references and index.
    Audience: Grades 4-6.
    ISBN 0-7565-1638-2 (hard cover : alk. paper)
    1. Adventure stories—Authorship—Juvenile literature. I. Title.
PN3377.5.A37F37 2006
808.3'87—dc22   2005033653

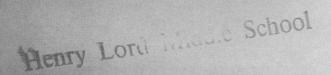

Your writing journey

Do you long to climb Himalayan peaks or discover lost cities in steamy Amazon forests? Could you survive on a desert island or drive a dogsled across Arctic tundra? Now is your chance to consider what such adventures might be like. Writing adventure stories, you can go anywhere and do anything in your imagination.

These stories have high stakes and lots of thrills. Often, the life of the hero hangs in the balance while he or she faces dangers posed by nature or threatening villains—or both. You will send characters on challenging journeys that test their bodies and their brains. Their main goal may be mere survival, or they may be after something precious—valuable treasures or personal freedom. This book won't tell you where to find the gold, but it will help you write action-packed stories.

CONTENTS

WANT TO BE A WRITER?

This book is the perfect place to start. It aims to give you the tools to write your own adventure-fiction stories. Learn how to craft believable characters, perfect plots, and satisfying beginnings, middles, and endings. Examples from famous books appear throughout, with tips and techniques from published authors to help you on your way.

Get the writing habit

Do timed and regular practice. Real writers learn to write even when they don't particularly feel like it.

Create a story-writing zone.

Keep a journal.

Keep a notebook—record interesting events and note how people behave and speak.

Generate ideas

Find a character whose story you want to tell. What is his or her problem?

Brainstorm to find out everything about your character.

Research settings, events, and other characters.

Get a mix of good and evil characters.

GETTING STARTED | SETTING THE SCENE | CHARACTERS | VIEWPOINT

You can follow your progress by using the bar located on the bottom of each page. The orange color tells you how far along the story-writing process you have gotten. As the blocks are filled out, your story will be growing.

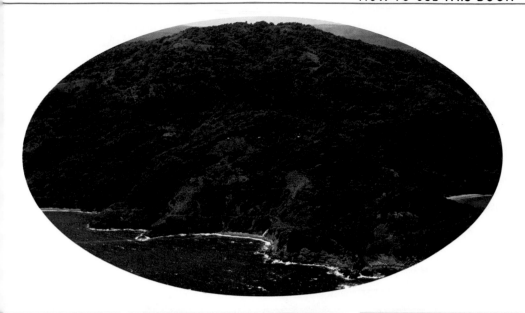

Plan

What is your story about?

What happens?

Plan beginning, middle, and end.

Write a synopsis or create story-boards.

Write

Write the first draft, then put it aside for a while.

Check spelling and dialogue—does it flow?

Remove unnecessary words.

Does the story have a good title and satisfying ending?

Avoid clichés.

Publish

Write or print the final draft.

Always keep a copy for yourself.

Send your story to children's magazines, Internet writing sites, competitions, or school magazines.

SYNOPSES AND PLOTS   WINNING WORDS   SCINTILLATING SPEECH   HINTS AND TIPS   THE NEXT STEP

When you get to the end of the bar, your book is ready to go! You are an author!
You now need to decide what to do with your book and what your next project should be.
Perhaps it will be a sequel to your story, or maybe something completely different.

BEGIN THE ADVENTURE

The first thing you need to do is gather your writing materials and set up your writing headquarters. As an adventure writer, you won't even need to leave your desk to have exciting times. All you need is a pen and paper to plot your gripping stories, and perhaps a computer to write the finished story.

Gather your tools

- a small notebook that you carry with you always
- lots of scrap paper and colored pencils for drawing maps and plans
- Post-it notes to keep track of vital information while you do your research

- stick-on stars for highlighting thoughts
- folders for stashing good story ideas
- dictionary, thesaurus, encyclopedia, and world atlas

Find a writing place

Finding a good place to write is very important. Your bedroom is probably the quietest place, and many famous writers do their best work in bedrooms, including Michael Morpurgo (author of *Kensuke's Kingdom*) and Morris Gleitzman (author of *Two Weeks with the Queen*). Gleitzman prefers to wear his pajamas when he sits at his computer. David Almond (author of *Kit's Wilderness*) does a lot of work on trains. So have fun discovering where your very best writing place might be. Maybe the museum or an Internet café has just the right atmosphere.

Create your story headquarters

• Play music from faraway places to help you create exotic locations.

• Put up travel posters of tropical islands, rain forests, and ancient ruins.

• Wear an adventure-writing hat (think Indiana Jones). You can make one or adapt one you already have.

• Choose special objects to have in your writing headquarters (HQ)—an African carving, a mysterious Chinese box— anything to stir your spirit of adventure.

Follow the writer's golden rule

Once you have chosen your writing space, the first step in becoming a writer is: Go there as often as possible and write. You must write and write regularly. This is the writer's golden rule.

Before you can set out for the Lost World of Imagination, you must start your writer's training. First, decide on the best time to do your writing practice. It could be 10 minutes a day before bedtime or an hour on Saturday.

Stick to it the same way you would practice a musical instrument. Then unlock your imagination with some timed brainstorming.

Now it's your turn

Free your creative thoughts

At practice time, have a pen and scrap paper ready. Sit in your writing HQ, close your eyes, and take four long, deep breaths to clear your mind. Now write "Treasure Island" at the top of the page. For two minutes, write all the adventure-related words and names that pop into your mind. Go. Go. Go! Don't think about it. Don't worry if the list is nonsense. Let words flow like an erupting volcano.

TIPS AND TECHNIQUES

Come stampeding elephants or plagues of locusts, make a date with your desk and stick to it.

Now it's your turn

Brainstorm your adventure setting

Take a look at what you wrote in the previous exercise. Circle five words that catch your eye. Give yourself 10 minutes to work them into a description of an exciting location—perhaps a desert island or a lost world. Again, write the first things you think of. Don't worry if they are nonsense. This is about becoming a writer, not about being a perfect writer.

When you have finished both practice exercises, give yourself a gold star. You are on your way to the Lost World of Imagination. The more you practice, the easier it will be to overcome the Story Spoiler, or internal critic—the voice in your head that always finds fault with your writing.

Brainstorm ideas

Try these story lines:

• You thought you were alone on the desert island, but one day when you went to the beach, you found a footprint.

• You are the sole survivor in a crashed plane on a desolate mountain.

Brainstorming with a friend can be fun. Try writing alternate lines of a story starting with:

• Through the jungle trees loomed a crumbling ruin hung with vines and ...

Case study

Kate DiCamillo was inspired to write by reading the children's books in the bookshop where she worked. Every day, she set her alarm for 4 A.M. so she could spend time writing before she went to work. Her hard work paid off when her first book, Because of Winn-Dixie, *became an award-winning success.*

BECOME ADVENTUROUS

All good writing starts with lots of good reading. Try to read as much as possible. Most adventures involve a quest, often in an exotic setting. The heroes must struggle against all sorts of hazards. Engaging, daring characters—such as Mark Twain's Huckleberry Finn or Joan Aiken's Dido Twite—and plenty of exciting action are the keys to a good adventure story.

Go on an adventure

Adventure writing is a popular type of fiction for readers of all ages. These stories put characters in situations that demand quick thinking, physical endurance, and determination. Often these stories focus on a character's quest for survival or search for some sort of reward, ranging from lost treasure to personal freedom. In the end, adventure stories often lead their heroes to a new confidence and independence, regardless of whether they find a fortune in lost treasure.

Read, read, read

The more you read, the easier it will be to decide what kind of stories you want to write. You could start with classic adventures like Robert Louis Stevenson's *Treasure Island* or Jack London's *White Fang*. Or you could choose modern stories like Gary Paulsen's *Hatchet* and Carl Hiaasen's fast-paced *Hoot*, a quest to save the breeding ground of some rare owls.

GETTING STARTED   SETTING THE SCENE   CHARACTERS   VIEWPOINT

Discover your tastes

As you read, think about why you like some stories more than others. Do you prefer ripping tales like the *Indiana Jones* films? Or do you prefer stories with a ring of truth like Lucy Jane Bledsoe's *Tracks in the Snow*? Keep a log of each book you read.

Look more deeply

Go back to your favorite adventure story. When you first read it, you probably lost yourself in it completely, just as the writer intended. Now reread it and ask yourself how the writer created such a believable and exciting story. This is another important step in learning to be a writer.

Now it's your turn

Brainstorm

Write "Desert Island" in the middle of an empty page. Then spend two minutes writing around it all the thoughts that a desert island brings to mind—think of barren sands, rolling waves, and mysterious sounds. Do frightening things live there? Write your first thoughts.

TIPS AND TECHNIQUES

As you read, think about your own story. Draw your characters and lost treasures or cities. Read some ancient adventures, too. The legend of King Arthur might give you an idea for a modern version of the story.

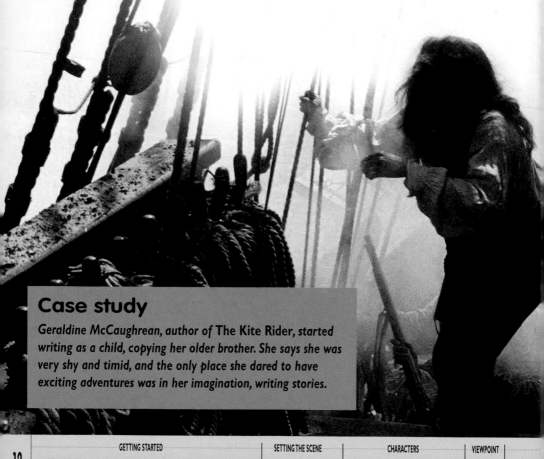

FIND YOUR VOICE

You've discovered that becoming a good writer means being a good reader. This is the only way to discover your own writer's voice—a style of writing that is uniquely yours. It is not something you learn quickly, which is why writing practice is so important. Writers go on developing their voices all their lives.

Find your writer's voice

Once you start reading with a writer's mind, you will notice that writers have their own rhythm and range of language. For instance, Sharon Creech (author of *The Wanderer*) sounds nothing like Michael Morpurgo (author of *Kensuke's Kingdom*). Spotting how different writers craft their stories is like learning to recognize different kinds of music.

Case study

Geraldine McCaughrean, author of The Kite Rider, started writing as a child, copying her older brother. She says she was very shy and timid, and the only place she dared to have exciting adventures was in her imagination, writing stories.

WRITERS' VOICES

**Look at the kinds of words these authors use.
Do they use lots of adjectives? Are they good ones?
What about the length of their sentences? Do some
styles seem old-fashioned? Do you think this matters?**

Robert Louis Stevenson

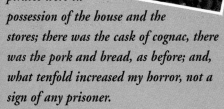

The glare of the torch, lighting up the interior of the block-house, showed me the worst of my apprehensions realized. The pirates were in possession of the house and the stores; there was the cask of cognac, there was the pork and bread, as before; and, what tenfold increased my horror, not a sign of any prisoner.

Robert Louis Stevenson, *Treasure Island*

Celia Rees

The deck swirled with smoke; it was like fighting in a fog. There was no time to draw a pistol, and guns are useless at close quarters. We had to slash our way back to our own ship.

Celia Rees, *Pirates!*

H. Rider Haggard

On we tramped silently as shades through the night and in the heavy sand. The karoo bushes caught our feet and retarded us, and the sand worked into our veldschoens and Good's shooting-boots, so that every few miles we had to stop and empty them.

H. Rider Haggard, *King Solomon's Mines*

Sharon Creech

We were racing along and it felt so terrific, all that wind! We had our foul-weather gear on, so we didn't mind the torrents of rain beating down as we plowed through the water.

Sharon Creech, *The Wanderer*

The ideas for adventure stories are everywhere. You may find them in old photographs, newspaper articles, or museum displays. Writers collect story snippets, and so do you—although you may not realize it. Locked away in your mind is a treasure trove of story ideas.

Access your story files

When writers are planning a story, they sift through their idea files. These could be notebooks, doodles, or story fragments already written. They also sift through their memories. But if you are stuck for ideas, timed brainstorming is a good way to access your mental story files. By writing down your first thoughts, you may set free some good ideas. Even if you do not spot them now, you may use them later.

Case Study

Michael Morpurgo bases all of his fiction on real-life situations. He says, "All my stories are based on truth of some sort, some nugget of reality. I need to have a face I recognize and put it in a book. I need to hear language. I need to have gone to the place about which I am writing."

TIPS AND TECHNIQUES

Keep your brainstorming results in a special notebook or file. They may seem like nonsense now, but the next time you flip through them, something may inspire you. You can brainstorm anywhere— when you are on the bus or even waiting for the dentist.

Make lists—mental ones if you have no paper—such as: How many words mean lost? How many ways are there to describe a jungle? What are some exotic place names? Who are my favorite heroes?

Exercises like this shake up your memories. Who knows what will pop out?

GETTING STARTED · SETTING THE SCENE · CHARACTERS · VIEWPOINT

What if?

A good way to imagine a story is to ask "what if" questions. Writers do this all the time; they see a situation and mix it with their imaginations. For instance, if a writer sees a child crying at the airport, he or she might ask: What if the child is being kidnapped? This seed of an idea might be used by the writer right away or stored for later. Kate DiCamillo discovered the idea for her book *The Tiger Rising* from a character in a short story she had written. She said the character kept hanging around in her imagination, and he finally told her that he knew where there was a tiger.

Now it's your turn

Use your imagination

In three minutes, brainstorm a list of as many "what if" situations as you can think of. For example: What if my family went on a sailing trip and I was washed overboard in a storm? What if I got home from school and found my parents had been kidnapped? What if my parents lost me as a baby and I was brought up by wolves?

Find more ideas and develop your story

Smart adventurers don't take unnecessary risks. They study the land, weigh the dangers, and take some expert advice before setting off into the wilderness. Writing an adventure is just the same. If you want to set your story in the Arctic, you need to know what it's like out there. Jack London, for instance, wrote *White Fang* and *The Call of the Wild* from firsthand experience. These would be good sources for you to use.

Use facts

Researching the background details for an adventure story can be like a history and geography assignment rolled into one. You don't have to know absolutely everything, but you need to know enough to see how the local details might affect your hero's story.

Study real-life adventures

• Read *National Geographic* magazine and explorers' own accounts of their journeys.

• Watch documentaries about earthquakes, volcano eruptions, and other disasters.

• Search media Web sites like CNN for exciting stories.

Make use of your own experiences

Holidays, school trips, and outdoor recreation will give you plenty of background material for a story. Keep a diary of all your experiences and record lots of details: colors, smells, sounds, how people behave, and so forth. Describe exactly how you feel, too. This is all part of your writer's training and could give you valuable raw material.

Case study

Real-life accounts are a gift for writers. Daniel Defoe based Robinson Crusoe on the shipwreck experiences of Alexander Selkirk, who told the writer the story of his desert-island survival.

Now it's your turn

Get a setting

Once your story ideas start simmering, you can help them along by describing the setting in detail. For 10 minutes, brainstorm everything you know about the setting. Make notes under the headings landscape, vegetation, wildlife, and climate. As you write, imagine being there. This will help bring your story to life.

Check out your computer games

If you like computer games, you'll know all about the character histories or back stories that brief you before you start a game. Video game fans often discuss what makes a good game—interesting characters, plenty of action, and an exciting climax, which are the same ingredients that writers need for their stories. Use some game ideas to help plot your own story.

TIPS AND TECHNIQUES

Story ideas can crop up anytime and anywhere. Always have a pen and notebook handy so you can write them down as soon as possible.

Case study

Robert Louis Stevenson's idea for Treasure Island began with a map of an island that he drew for his stepson. Stevenson was optimistic that the story would be a success, declaring, "If this don't fetch the kids, why, they have gone rotten since my day."

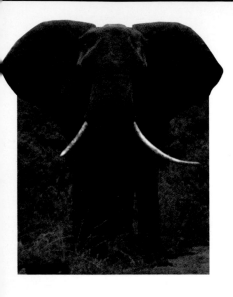

DESCRIBE YOUR WORLD

In adventure stories, the natural world may have a big part to play when you devise your plot. It can provide a host of scary hazards for your heroes to tackle—charging elephants, sandstorms, or volcanic eruptions. The more specific you can be, the more thrilling the scenes. Research carefully and be accurate with details.

Build your landscape in detail

• To create exotic settings, use travel guidebooks for specific information.

• Study *National Geographic* location photographs. Imagine yourself stepping inside them, and write down what it might feel like.

• Type your location into an Internet search engine. There may be travelers' photos and diary entries or exciting travel articles on a Web site.

• Read lots of fictional stories set in similar places.

TIPS AND TECHNIQUES

When creating your setting, focus on details that will affect your characters and plot. Check your facts. Find out what an earthquake is really like, or learn how a charging elephant really behaves before you include one of them in a story.

Get your hero's reaction to the location

In *Kensuke's Kingdom*, Michael Morpurgo describes only island details that dramatically affect the castaway. There are the shrieking gibbons that he hears when he first wakes on the island: "The howling became a fearful crescendo of screeching that died away in its own echoes." Nightly mosquito attacks add to his desperation: "From dusk onwards they searched me out, buzzed in on me and ate me alive. There was no hiding-place. My nights were one long torture, and in the morning I would scratch myself raw."

Use what you know

Your setting could be somewhere that you know well. If so, focus on things about it that will work well for your plot—as Carl Hiaasen does in *Hoot,* set in his home state of Florida. From the school bus, newcomer Roy sees a strange barefoot boy sprinting along the streets:

> *Maybe he's still running, Roy thought as he ate lunch. Florida was made for running; Roy had never seen anyplace so flat. Back in Montana you had steep craggy mountains that rose ten thousand feet into the clouds. Here the only hills were man-made highway bridges—smooth, gentle slopes of concrete.*
>
> Carl Hiaasen, *Hoot*

Now it's your turn

Consider a tourist's view

Look over the two sets of brainstormed notes about your exciting location. Now imagine you own some kind of wilderness camp there. You need more visitors to come. For 15 minutes, brainstorm a short tourist guide that you hope will attract them. When you have finished, start a new piece of paper. This time, you are an angry tourist writing a letter of complaint to the camp manager. For 15 minutes, list all the horrible things that happened to you there.

Just write down your first thoughts.

Read through both versions. Does the place seem real to you?
Have you spotted some good hazards to use in your story?
If so, it's time to think about how to describe them.

Adventures are all about action, and too much description slows the pace. Make the setting work for your story. In a jungle adventure, for example, you could show your heroes dripping in sweat or side-stepping snakes. Then drop them into a swamp.

Good setting: Recipe 1

Show the scene from a character's point of view. Here Jim Hawkins prepares to land on Treasure Island. His description suggests treasure and also a chilling sense of being stranded:

The whole anchorage had fallen into shadow—the last rays, I remember, falling through a glade of the wood, and shining bright as jewels, on the flowery mantle of the wreck. It began to be chill; the tide was rapidly fleeting seaward, the schooner settling more and more on her beam-ends.

Robert Louis Stevenson, *Treasure Island*

Good setting: Recipe 2

Combine description with a dramatic event:

Somewhere out there in the snow, screened from his sight by trees and thickets, Henry knew that the wolf-pack, One Ear and Bill were coming together. He heard a shot, then two shots in rapid succession, and he knew that Bill's ammunition was gone. Then he heard a great outcry of snarls and yelps. He recognized One Ear's yell of pain and terror, and he heard a wolf-cry that bespoke a stricken animal. And that was all. The snarls ceased. The yelping died away. Silence settled down again on the lonely land.

Jack London, *White Fang*

Good setting: Recipe 3

Trigger the senses. In *Pirates!* Nancy and Minerva escape to the
Jamaican highlands:

*We found a series of mist-filled ravines, with cloudy vapor escaping
in ragged wisps, like steam from a lidded cauldron. We rode with our
heads pressed to our horses necks, into dense dripping trees swathed
with moss and hanging vines and spiky-leafed
dangling plants that seemed to feed only on air.*
Celia Rees, *Pirates!*

Now it's your turn

Exciting openings

You may not have a complete story idea, but
using your three sets of exciting location notes,
write an opening scene of about 200 words.
Combine sharp details of your location with
some action. Maybe your hero is dodging a
bear in the forest or being stalked by some thugs
through an abandoned factory. Or perhaps your
story starts just as a huge wave washes your hero
off a ship. Try to add some mystery or drama.
What is your character feeling in your location?

TIPS AND TECHNIQUES

*When using description in an adventure, say just enough
to move the story forward. If you say too much, the story
will sink like an overloaded canoe. Try to mesh the
description with some action, as in the Pirates! example.*

DISCOVER YOUR HERO

When it comes to creating an adventure hero (protagonist), there are plenty of models to choose from, from Robin Hood to Lara Croft. Whoever your hero is, you must care for him or her and show why.

Find a good name

Give your hero the perfect name, and he or she could spring into life. Make it snappy, with a certain style. Scan your dictionary, phone book, or atlas for ideas. Now meet Beatrice Leep living up to her name:

> *It wasn't Mr. Ryan who'd saved Roy from a whupping in the closet; it was Beatrice Leep. She had left Dana Matherson stripped down to his underpants and trussed to the flagpole in front of the administration building at Trace Middle School. There, Beatrice had "borrowed" a bicycle, forcefully installed Roy on the handlebars, and was now churning at a manic pace towards an unknown destination.*
> Carl Hiaasen, *Hoot*

Build a picture

What does your hero look like? Think about the person's build, appearance, and clothing. What are your hero's likes and dislikes? Think about his or her strengths and, more importantly, weaknesses. These could make your story more dramatic because your hero will have to confront his or her weaknesses. Perfect heroes are dull.

Give your hero a past

Your hero had a life before the story began, and his or her history will affect how he or she acts. Sum it up briefly so it doesn't slow the story:

> *Kim was English. Though he was burned black as any native; though he spoke the vernacular by preference, and his mother-tongue in clipped uncertain sing-song; though he consorted on terms of equality with the small boys of the bazaar; Kim was white—a poor white of the very poorest.*
>
> Rudyard Kipling, *Kim*

Tell your hero's problems

All good stories are about heroes struggling to solve their problems. Adventurers are often misfits, too. For instance, Lila, in Philip Pullman's *The Firework-Maker's Daughter*, longs to be a firework maker like her father, but he won't reveal the final secret of his trade because Lila is a girl.

Now it's your turn

Create characters

Take a large sheet of paper, leave a left-hand margin, and divide the page into 36 boxes— six across the top and six down. Write these headings down the margin: looks, always wears, always acts, is good at, is bad at, favorite things. Now take one minute to write in the top row of boxes the first six things you can think of about your hero's looks, such as a scar on the nose, a lizard tattoo on the wrist, and so on. Repeat this for the other categories. You will soon know 36 things about your hero.

Now, for 10 minutes, pour out your feelings about yourself: How did you feel when you aced a test or climbed a mountain? How did you feel when you tripped on the last hurdle or were cut from the team? Everyone has successes and failures, and they are all raw material for your hero's strengths and weaknesses.

All adventure stories need antagonists to challenge the heroes. These can be natural enemies—sea storms, breaking dams, great white sharks—human enemies, or both. To add as much excitement as possible, you need to show why these opponents are so dangerous.

Find a motive

If your story has a human villain, find out what makes him or her bad. In treasure hunts, the villains are likely to be driven by greed. But the best villains need more than one flaw to make them convincing. When you create your own villains, don't be too obvious. Think sneaky, too. Perhaps your hero thinks the villain is a friend. Maybe the villain is very charming. If the villain is a bully, remember there are all sorts of bullies, from a cruel pirate leader to a school thug. If an active volcano serves as the villain, build up the hazards piece by piece; mirror the sense of pressure inside the volcano before it blows. In other words, give the volcano a personality.

Literary villains

LONG JOHN SILVER IN *TREASURE ISLAND*

Long John Silver seems friendly when Jim Hawkins first sees him at the Spy-Glass Tavern:

> His left leg was cut off close by the hip, and under his left shoulder he carried a crutch, which he managed with wonderful dexterity, hopping upon it like a bird. He was tall and strong, with a face as big as a ham—plain and pale, but intelligent and smiling.
>
> Robert Louis Stevenson, *Treasure Island*

BARTHOLOME THE BRAZILIAN

In Pirates! *Bartholome is a buccaneer turned Jamaican plantation owner. When Nancy Kington meets him at her father's funeral, we know at once that he will become a serious threat to her:*

> He took my hand. His long fingers were heavy with rings, square-cut rubies and emeralds. He stood looking down at me with eyes so black as to show no pupil. They held a gleam of red, almost purple, like overripe cherries, or deadly nightshade berries.
>
> Celia Rees, *Pirates!*

GAGOOL IN *KING SOLOMON'S MINES*

Gagool is the aged witchdoctor in service to wicked King Twala. She is set to kill Allan Quartermain and his friends:

> Nearer and nearer waltzed Gagool looking for the world like an animated crooked stick or comma, her horrid eyes gleaming and glowing with a most unholy luster.
>
> H. Rider Haggard, *King Solomon's Mines*

TIPS AND TECHNIQUES

Villains will have weaknesses. In The Mummy, Benny's greed leaves him trapped forever in the City of the Dead. And don't forget: Sometimes villains have good sides, too.

DEVELOP A SUPPORTING CAST

Adventurers—from Indiana Jones to Alex Rider—are often loners. But to develop them as rounded characters that readers want to read about, you must show how they behave with other people. This is why supporting characters are so important. They help to reveal the different sides of your hero, and they may also show the villain's true nature.

TIPS AND TECHNIQUES

Show—don't tell. Instead of telling readers that your hero is kind-hearted, show him being kind-hearted in a scene with a minor character. In David Almond's Kit's Wilderness, *we learn a lot about Kit by seeing how he behaves with his grandfather, whom Kit fears is dying. We see how much Kit loves him.*

Now it's your turn

Discover unique qualities

Focus on your supporting characters. What are their special characteristics: their looks, the way they speak, their odd habits? Think how they could help or harm your hero. Imagine you are a team leader, recruiting members for an expedition. Interview the candidates. Look for those with the qualities you most need.

Reveal true character

In *The Great Elephant Chase* by Gillian Cross, the hero Tad is treated like a dimwit, and even Tad believes this view of himself, until the elephant starts to change his ideas:

[Tad] was being teased. There was no mistaking it. ... Khush squirted again, with a perfect aim. Never hitting Tad's feet, but always close enough to make him jump away. When Tad had been teased at school, it was always meant unkindly. ... This game was gentle and amicable, and for a moment he was completely bewildered by it. Then, suddenly, he imagined how the two of them must look ... [and] started to laugh.
Gillian Cross, *The Great Elephant Chase*

Make them real

Your story's minor characters won't be as developed—or, as deeply detailed—as your hero and villain, but they must seem real. A good way to bring them to life is to give them one or two memorable characteristics, such as Mahbub Ali's bright red beard in Rudyard Kipling's *Kim*.

CHOOSE A POINT OF VIEW

Before you start to write your story, you must decide whose point of view you want to show. Will you write from your hero's point of view, or do you want to describe everything that happens to all your characters?

Decide on your point of view
The omniscient

Traditional tales use the omniscient or all-seeing viewpoint. This tells readers all that is going on in a scene in a rather detached way, like a filmmaker shooting a movie.

TIPS AND TECHNIQUES

When you write from your character's viewpoint, you must look through his or her eyes, feel what he or she feels, and hear what he or she hears. It's a bit like acting.

A second cry arose, piercing the silence with needle-like shrillness. Both men located the sound. It was to the rear, somewhere in the snow expanse they had just traversed. A third and answering cry arose, also to the rear and to the left of the second cry.

"They're after us, Bill," said the man at the front. His voice sounded hoarse and unreal, and he had spoken with apparent effort.

"Meat is scarce," answered his comrade. "I ain't seen a rabbit sign for days."

Jack London, *White Fang*

Third-person viewpoint

Writing from only one character's point of view is called the third-person viewpoint. It is usually written in the past tense. It takes us right inside the character's head and involves us more closely. For example, the Jack London excerpt might go something like this:

"Bill's heart jumped. A second cry! It pierced the silence with needle-like shrillness. He swung around to locate it. It's behind us, he thought, back on our trail. Then from the front of the sled he heard Henry mutter, his voice hoarse, 'They're after us, Bill.' Bill grunted, struggling to hide his own fear. 'Meat is scarce,' he said. 'I ain't seen a rabbit for days.'"

First-person viewpoint

The first-person viewpoint, using "I" or "we," is closest to the spoken word. It is intimate and exciting. Your characters will be revealing their innermost thoughts. You can use straight narrative (storytelling), letters, e-mails, or diary entries. The disadvantage is that you can only reveal other characters' views when recording their speech in dialogue or reporting on their behavior.

Now it's your turn

Change viewpoints

Take 30 minutes to write a short action scene between your hero and villain. First, write it from the omniscient or all-seeing viewpoint. Next, write it from your hero's viewpoint and then from the villain's. Experiment with the first person and the present tense, too. Read your efforts aloud to yourself. Which version do you prefer and why?

TELL YOUR STORY'S STORY

As your story firms up in your mind, it's a good idea to describe it in two or three paragraphs. This is called a synopsis. An editor often likes to see a synopsis before accepting a story for publication, but don't give away the ending.

Study back cover blurbs

Study the blurbs on the covers of some adventure stories. See how they say just enough about the hero and his or her problems to make the reader want to find out more. They also convey tone, showing whether the book is serious or humorous. Here is the witty blurb from Zizou Corder's *Lionboy*:

"Charlie Ashanti speaks Cat. He takes it for granted—but when his mum and dad go missing, the cats are the only friends he can turn to. Setting out to find his parents, Charlie stows away on an incredible circus ship bound for Paris. On board he meets six proud, beautiful lions who need his help. With danger close behind and uncertainty ahead, they embark together on the adventure of a lifetime."

The back cover of *The Great Elephant Chase* by Gillian Cross conjures up a sense of great adventure and drama:

"I'm not going to wait around here and let Mr. Jackson steal my elephant." Penniless and parentless, Tad and Cissie are on the run from the tyrannical Mr. Jackson. But hiding an enormous elephant is no easy task, and Tad realizes that he must find courage and determination if they are ever to reach their destination—a proper home on the other side of America.

Make a story map

By now you have created a setting, a cast of characters, and a synopsis that says what your story is about. The next thing to do is to make a story map or storyboard to stop you from losing track of the plot.

Plan your story in scenes

Before filmmakers start filming, they sketch out the main story episodes in a series of storyboards. This helps them figure out how best to shoot each scene. You can do this for your story. Draw the main story events in pictures and add a few notes to describe each scene.

TIPS AND TECHNIQUES

If you can't say what your story is about in a sentence or two, it is probably too complicated. Simplify it. Ask yourself: Whose story is this, and what is the best way to tell it? Think about your theme, too. Adventure themes might be proving one's worth, overcoming hardship, mustering courage, developing friendships, challenging evil, or surviving difficult circumstances.

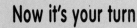

Now it's your turn

Write your blurb

Try to sum up your story in a single striking sentence, then develop it into two or three short paragraphs. Think about your potential readers and look for ways to make them want to find out more.

TELL YOUR STORY'S STORY

Create a synopsis

Before novelists start writing, they often list all their chapters and tell briefly what will happen in each episode. This is called a chapter synopsis, and it provides a writer with a skeleton for the plot. Like the general synopsis, it helps keep the story on track during the writing process.

A famous example

Here are some storyboard captions for *King Solomon's Mines* by H. Rider Haggard.

1. Game-hunter Allan Quartermain agrees to guide Sir Henry Curtis to the fabled King Solomon's Mines to find his lost brother. Captain Good accompanies them.
2. A mysterious Zulu, Umbopa, joins their party.
3. The party makes a dangerous trek across desert and mountains to Kukuanaland, which is ruled by the wicked King Twala and his ancient, evil witchdoctor, Gagool.
4. Umbopa tells Quartermain that Twala seized the throne by killing his father. Umbopa is really Ignosi, the true king.
5. Quartermain's party helps Ignosi regain his rightful throne.
6. Ignosi spares Gagool so she can guide Quartermain to the mines to complete his quest.
7. Everyone is trapped in the treasure chamber; Gagool is crushed to death by a secret rock door.
8. Everyone escapes through dark passages with only a few diamonds.
9. They say farewell to King Ignosi.
10. Sir Henry's brother is discovered at an oasis on the trek home.

Novel versus short story

King Solomon's Mines is a novel, but mapping out the main scenes like this can help you write a short story, too, and can keep you focused on the main character and on the most exciting events. Short stories usually have only one or two well-developed characters and a single story line, whereas novels may have many characters and several subplots besides the main story.

Build a novel

If you choose to write a novel, a chapter synopsis will help you map out a more complex plot and decide which characters you are likely to need to best tell your story. When you start to write, each chapter will unfold like a mini-story inside the larger story. Each chapter will have a beginning, middle, and end, and will carry the narrative forward by adding intriguing details and episodes to entice readers and involve them ever more deeply in your story. In a novel, there is much more room to develop your characters and more opportunity for action scenes and plot twists.

TIPS AND TECHNIQUES

Don't let a novel's length discourage you from writing one. If you use the storyboard approach, it can be easier to write a novel than it is to write a good short story.

Now it's your turn

Sketch your hero

If you are struggling to work out your storyboard, try this exercise:

1. At the top of a large piece of paper, sketch your hero or write his or her name.

2. Now ask the hero what his or her problems are. List the answers underneath and draw a circle around them.

3. Next ask what your hero wants or needs to do to solve these problems. Write or draw these answers inside a circle at the bottom of the page.

4. Finally, ask your hero what people, places, or things stand in the way of achieving his or her goal. Draw these in the middle of the page. As you do this, start asking how your hero intends to overcome these obstacles. What will happen if your hero fails? What's at stake? Give yourself 20 minutes to do this exercise.

You have planned your plot and are ready to start telling your story. Your first task is to grab your readers' interest. How will you win them to your hero's cause?

Hook your readers

Story beginnings have many important jobs to do—setting the scene, introducing the main characters, revealing their problems and conflicts, and sending them on their way to resolve their difficulties. But where do you start the story? One way is to leap in at a crisis point. In *Hoot*, Carl Hiaasen begins:

"Roy would not have noticed the strange boy if it weren't for Dana Matherson."

Instantly there are questions: Who is Roy? What sort of strange boy did he see? How did Dana Matherson cause Roy to notice the boy?

In *The Firework-Maker's Daughter*, Philip Pullman (left) humorously reworks a traditional fairy-tale beginning:

"A thousand miles ago, in a country east of the jungle and south of the mountains, there lived a Firework Maker called Lalchand and his daughter Lila."

TIPS AND TECHNIQUES

When you have decided on the opening scene, start work on a mind-grabbing first sentence. For more ideas, use your library to study first sentences. Write down your favorites. Write and rewrite your own until you are absolutely happy with it.

Draw the readers in by:

Creating mystery

No one believed Amy was missing. Mom and Dad, busy getting ready for work, were angry about the weather, which was turning bad in time for the weekend. It was April, which meant it should have been spring. But we live in a small town in the Sierra mountains of California. Up here you can't count on spring until June. On this Friday morning, flat, grayish snow clouds hung over our world.

Lucy Jane Bledsoe, *Tracks in the Snow*

Making characters intriguing

I write for many reasons. I write, not least to quiet my grief. I find that by reliving the adventures that I shared with Minerva, I can lessen the pain of our parting. I must find new diversions that fit my station now that I have put up my pistols and cutlass and have exchanged my breeches for a dress.

Celia Rees, *Pirates!*

Adding humor

The Queen looked out across the Mudford's living room and wished everyone a happy Christmas. Colin scowled. Easy for you, he thought. Bet you got what you wanted. Bet if you wanted a microscope you got a microscope. Bet your tree was covered with microscopes.

Morris Gleitzman,
Two Weeks with the Queen

Being dramatic

I disappeared on the night before my twelfth birthday. July 28, 1988. Only now can I at last tell the whole extraordinary story, the true story. Kensuke made me promise that I would say nothing, nothing at all, until at least ten years had passed.

Michael Morpurgo,
Kensuke's Kingdom

Once you have caught your readers' interests, you must find ways to keep turning up the tension. Add complications. Increase the conflict. Build suspense between the characters and excitement at a relentless pace.

Keep moving

Keep your characters engaged with their quest, always on the move, working things out, coming to wrong conclusions, having fights, or escaping disasters.

Develop a subplot

In *Lionboy*, by Zizou Corder, the main story is about Charlie trying to find his kidnapped parents. Hot on their trail, he stows away on a circus ship, where he meets six lions. Able to speak their language, he promises to help them return to Africa. Now he has to find his parents and keep his promise to the lions.

Expose the weaknesses

Don't forget your hero's weaknesses. If your hero is short-tempered or rash, he or she might play into the villain's hands. Reckless curiosity can land your hero in trouble.

Add drama

Think hard about your supporting characters, too. They could add some drama. Are there simmering jealousies, acts of betrayal, or simple misunderstandings that could make things tougher for the hero?

Create a time challenge

In *The Great Elephant Chase*, by Gillian Cross, Tad and Cissie are on the run from the dreadful Mr. Jackson with Khush the elephant. They have to keep on the move, but how can they make an elephant go faster when his feet are sore?

Fake it

You can create suspense with a false happy ending. For a blissful moment, the hero thinks he or she has won, but just when your hero's guard is down, the problems come roaring back—bigger and bolder—and the challenge begins again.

Now it's your turn

Find weaknesses

Focus on your hero's weaknesses. For five minutes, write your first thoughts on how these might complicate and add drama to your story. Perhaps your hero refuses to see some important truth; perhaps he or she is a bad judge of character, and a friend turns out to have doubtful motives. Think how these factors might bring your story to a climax.

SYNOPSES AND PLOTS · · · · · WINNING WORDS · · · · · SCINTILLATING SPEECH · · · · · HINTS AND TIPS · · · · · THE NEXT STEP

37

END WITH A BANG

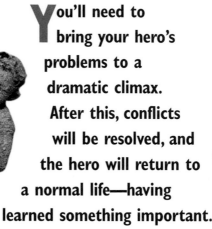

You'll need to bring your hero's problems to a dramatic climax. After this, conflicts will be resolved, and the hero will return to a normal life—having learned something important.

Conclude your adventure

Most readers like some sort of happy ending, but it is best to avoid the traditional happily-ever-after approach. Your adventure story ending will need to be more realistic. Your hero has probably survived a tough situation and gained a lot in the process. He or she might have lost something, too—perhaps a good friend. Or he or she might have had to learn a hard truth. In other words, your hero will be older and wiser. In *Hatchet*, by Gary Paulsen, a plane crash leaves Brian alone in the wilderness. At the beginning of the book, he doesn't know what to do and feels sorry for himself, but as the story progresses, Brian learns how to do things like build fires and find food. At the end of the story, Brian is able to use his senses and enjoy the wonders of nature all around him.

Avoid bad endings

Bad endings are those that:

• are too grim and leave the readers with no hope

• fail to show how the characters have changed

• fizzle out because you've run out of ideas

USE DRAMATIC DIALOGUE

Dialogue lets readers "hear" your characters' own voices. It breaks pages of solid print and gives readers eyes a rest. When done well, dialogue can add color, pace, mood, and suspense to a story.

et characters speak for themselves

he best way to learn about dialogue is to switch on your listening ear and eavesdrop. Listen to e way people phrase their sentences. Write down any good expressions. Did someone say "I'm cked off" instead of "I'm angry"? Watch people's body language when they are whispering or rguing. Look, listen, and absorb.

Now it's your turn

Stand out

Tune in to a TV talk show. Spend 10 minutes writing down exactly what people say—including all the ums, ers, and repetitions. Listen for a range of voices: young, old, smart, foolish, angry, or cheery. Next compare it with some dialogue in a book. You will see at once that written dialogue does not include all the hesitations of natural speech, but it gives an impression of how people speak to one another.

Now it's your turn

Rewrite an ending

Read the ending of your favorite adventure story. Are there other endings it could have had? Write one of them. Put it aside. Go back and read both versions later. Now which ending do you prefer, and why?

Have the last laugh

In *Two Weeks with the Queen,* Morris Gleitzman begins and ends with a wry joke about the Queen of England. These provide a comic frame for hero Colin's serious quest to find the world's best doctor to cure his brother. The final joke is the ultimate in upbeat endings. Read the book to find out why.

Create mixed emotions

The last lines of Anthony Horowitz's *Stormbreaker* have a dramatic, filmlike quality. Alex Rider watches the man who killed his uncle depart. His feelings are very mixed. Alex has solved the mystery, but he has not found the justice he craves. What other emotions does this ending evoke?

> *Behind the glass, [the assassin] raised his hand. A gesture of friendship? A salute? Alex raised his hand. The helicopter spun away. Alex stood where he was, watching it, until it had disappeared in the dying light.*
>
> Anthony Horowitz, *Stormbreaker*

TIPS AND TECHNIQUES

Good stories may seem to go in straight lines—beginning, middle, and end—but they also go around in circles. The hero returns to the place where he or she started but is now wiser.

42

GETTING STARTED   SETTING THE SCENE   CHARACTERS   VIEWPOINT   SYNOPSES AND PLOTS   WINNING WORDS   SCINTILLATING SPEECH   HINTS AND TIPS   THE NEXT STEP

39

MAKE YOUR WORDS WORK

Words are valuable things. Like water on a desert trek, you should use them sparingly and make every one count. In action-packed adventures, every word must work hard to carry the story forward.

Use vivid imagery

Metaphors and similes help readers to see a scene swiftly. In *King Solomon's Mines*, H. Rider Haggard uses a metaphor to describe some giraffes "which galloped or rather sailed off." In *Hoot*, Carl Hiaasen uses a simile, then a metaphor: "His legs felt like wet cement, and his lungs were on fire." In *The Kite Rider*, Geraldine McCaughrean uses the same idea as both a simile and a metaphor: "Jealousy, like a badly lit firework, fizzled and fumed in Haoyou's guts." In *Two Weeks with the Queen,* by Morris Gleitzman, a comic scene is used to relieve a tragic mood. Colin has gotten some bad news, and he defuses his anger and sorrow among the doctors' cars in the hospital parking lot:

Ssssssssssssssssssss. Colin watched as the air hissed out of the tire of the Mercedes. ... How dare they drive cars with automatic aerials and dual anti-lock braking systems and wipers on the headlamps when they couldn't even cure cancer?

Morris Gleitzman, *Two Weeks with the Queen*

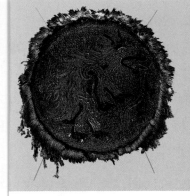

Work out with words

Give your vocabulary a workout. Brainstorm Come up with 30 adjectives and 30 nouns. Pa randomly and see what you get: a blue-eyed bo silken shield, or a frozen feather. Then reinvent sayings. Don't say something is as white as snow. white as a crocodile's grin or as an Arctic winter. dictionary, too, and play word games.

Write with bite

When writing action scenes, choose words that sound most like the action you are describ "smash" is more powerful than "hit," and "shriek" is more piercing than "cry."

Vary the length of your sentences, too. Try short ones for fast action and longer ones for lingering events.

Take a breath

Adventure stories are full of striving and struggling. Now and then, you need to give readers the chance to take a breather. Too much of anything can turn readers off. When they have had a break with some light relief, your return to your mai mood (whether it is action or tragedy) will be much more effective.

TIPS AND TECHNIQUES

Increase suspense by building to an exciting moment. Give readers hints of the danger to come and then pounce. Or use foreshadowing—drop clues in advance about possible hazards.

Now it's your turn

Self edit

Turn an overheard argument into a piece of fiction. Put all the anger into the spoken words. Don't rely on tags like "yelled" or "screamed" to show the mood. Use short, sharp bursts of speech. Now do a second draft and cut down the words to the bare bones. Give yourself a gold star. The art of editing your own work is an essential writing skill.

Follow convention

The way dialogue is written follows certain conventions or rules. It is common to start a new paragraph for every new speaker. What a speaker says is enclosed in quotation marks, followed by speech tags (such as "he said" or "she said"). Putting the speech tags in the middle of a line can give a sense of real conversation, as in this extract from *Stormbreaker* by Anthony Horowitz.

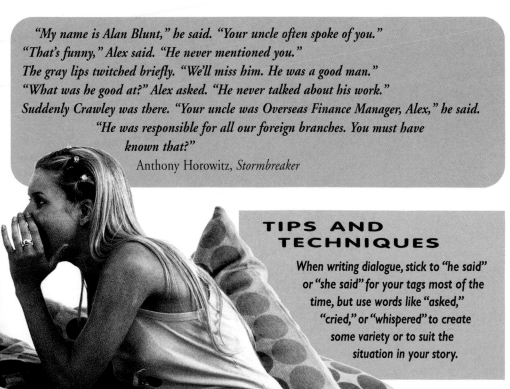

"My name is Alan Blunt," he said. "Your uncle often spoke of you."
"That's funny," Alex said. "He never mentioned you."
The gray lips twitched briefly. "We'll miss him. He was a good man."
"What was he good at?" Alex asked. "He never talked about his work."
Suddenly Crawley was there. "Your uncle was Overseas Finance Manager, Alex," he said.
"He was responsible for all our foreign branches. You must have known that?"
Anthony Horowitz, *Stormbreaker*

TIPS AND TECHNIQUES

When writing dialogue, stick to "he said" or "she said" for your tags most of the time, but use words like "asked," "cried," or "whispered" to create some variety or to suit the situation in your story.

USE DRAMATIC DIALOGUE

Write what they say

Details about a place or character can often be told much more quickly in a conversation. Readers learn from what the characters say, and the story moves on.

Create suspense

A scene can be written more humorously or dramatically in a series of spoken exchanges. In *Hoot*, Roy trails the running boy to his hideout, but when he opens a garbage bag, he finds himself in danger:

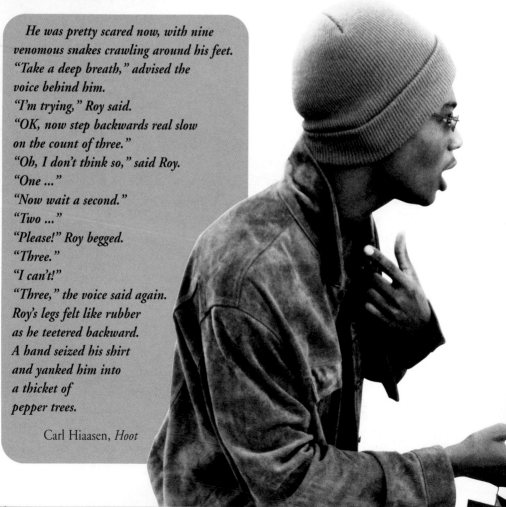

He was pretty scared now, with nine venomous snakes crawling around his feet.
"Take a deep breath," advised the voice behind him.
"I'm trying," Roy said.
"OK, now step backwards real slow on the count of three."
"Oh, I don't think so," said Roy.
"One ..."
"Now wait a second."
"Two ..."
"Please!" Roy begged.
"Three."
"I can't!"
"Three," the voice said again. Roy's legs felt like rubber as he teetered backward. A hand seized his shirt and yanked him into a thicket of pepper trees.

Carl Hiaasen, *Hoot*

Now it's your turn

Craft a conversation

Think of a scene where an explanation is needed—perhaps to account for your hero's behavior. Write it first as a piece of narrative to get down all the details. Then convey the same information as a conversation. Try to make the characters sound different from each other.

Show a character's opinions and viewpoints

If you are telling the story from your hero's viewpoint, dialogue is the only way for readers to hear directly from the other characters. In *The Kite Rider,* by Geraldine McCaughrean, the story is told from Haoyou's viewpoint. In the next excerpt, greedy Great-Uncle Bo has tracked him down and demands all his nephew's circus earnings:

TIPS AND TECHNIQUES

Dialogue can add drama if the characters lie. It can also be used to drop hints about dangers that lie ahead.

"Where's the money?"
"What money?"
"The gold the Khan gave you!"
"But—I was going to send it to my mother and Wawa!"
"Nonsense. I can put it to good use. I've made a wager."
He took Haoyou's hair and coaxed him out of the tent by it. Encouraged by Miao Jie's earlier talk of defiance, Haoyou dared to persist: "I want to send it home to Mother. It's special. From Tibet! I want her to see it!"
"Gold's gold," said Bo ...
"Now do as you are told."

Geraldine McCaughrean,
The Kite Rider

Use different voices

In the last exercise, you practiced creating different speakers. If you found it hard, don't worry—it is the most difficult thing for a writer to do. Even well-known writers aren't always good at writing dialogue. Remember, your characters won't necessarily speak like you.

Show social class

Curly, in Carl Hiaasen's *Hoot*, is the angry construction site foreman. He thinks he's caught Roy sabotaging the site. See how Hiaasen suggests that Curly isn't very well educated:

> *"What's your name? What're you doing here?" the foreman hollered.*
> *"This is private property, don't you know that? You wanna go to jail, junior?"*
> *Roy stopped pedaling and caught his breath.*
> *"I know what you're up to!" the bald man snarled. "I know your sneaky game."*
> *Roy said, "Please, mister, let me go. I was only feeding the owls."*
> *The crimson drained from the foreman's cheeks.*
> *"What owls?" he said, not so loudly. "There ain't no owls around here."*
> *"Oh, yes, there are," Roy said. "I've seen them."*
> *The bald guy looked extremely nervous and agitated. ... "Listen to me, boy. You didn't see no ... owls, OK? What you saw was a wild chicken!"*
>
> Carl Hiaasen, *Hoot*

TIPS AND TECHNIQUES

If your character has a foreign accent, don't attempt to replicate it exactly. Instead, find ways to suggest the accent only—either in the way the speech is phrased or in the occasional use of a dialect or foreign word, such as a greeting.

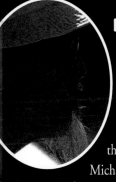

Non-native English speaker

Kensuke is a doctor who has been stranded on a desert island since the Second World War. Notice the respectful Japanese "san" attached to the end of Kensuke's version of Michael's name. Also, the opinions he expresses are characteristic of Asian philosophy:

"It is easier when you are old like me, Micasan," he said. *"What is?" I asked. "Waiting," he said. "One day a ship will come, Micasan. Maybe soon, maybe not so soon. But it will come. Life must not be spent always hoping, always waiting. Life is for living."*

Michael Morpurgo,
Kensuke's Kingdom

Regional accent

In the classic Mark Twain novel, *The Adventures of Tom Sawyer*, the Southern accent of Tom and his friend Huck is suggested by their broken sentences and use of words like "reckon" and "ain't." Here Tom and Huck discuss Muff Potter's trial:

"That's just the same way they go on round me. I reckon he's a goner. Don't you feel sorry for him, sometimes?"

"Most always—most always. He ain't no account; but then he hain't ever done anything to hurt anybody. Just fishes a little, to get money to get drunk on—and loafs around considerable; but lord, we all do that—leastways most of us—preachers and suchlike."

Mark Twain, *The Adventures of Tom Sawyer*

Now it's your turn

Expose the generation gap

Write down a conversation between you and one of your parents. Try to capture exactly how your parent speaks. What words or phrases does he or she always use? What expressions do you always use? When you have finished, rewrite the conversation, replacing one of the characters with a grandparent or older person. Are there more differences?

BEAT WRITER'S BLOCK

Even the most dogged adventurers run out of steam, and so can writers. They run out of words or the will to write. This is called writer's block. It can last for days or sometimes even longer. Here are some of the causes and how to overcome them.

Stop the Story Spoiler

Back on page 9, you read about the Story Spoiler—your internal critic that finds fault with everything you write and eventually drives you back to the TV. Do not listen! Think of yourself as a literary Indiana Jones, and show the Story Spoiler the bullwhip.

Uncover new ideas

Having nothing to say is a common excuse writers give for not writing. But if you have been doing your writing practice regularly and following the exercises, you will always find something to say. It doesn't matter how good or clever it is, just write it down. You will learn to write even when you don't feel inspired. Don't forget, ideas are everywhere.

Use rejection or criticism to your advantage

No one enjoys rejection and criticism, but learning to accept them is an important part of becoming a writer. If you ask someone to read your work, be prepared for negative comments. Consider both fair criticism and rejection as opportunities to improve your story.

Now it's your turn

Think positive thoughts

Write on the cover of your notebook, "Writing is an adventure. No one said it was easy." Brainstorm for five minutes. List all the things you find difficult about writing. Now list all the things you love about writing. Look over your list of difficulties. Consider them honestly. Are they things that can be fixed with more practice and more reading? Is learning to write more important to you than the problems? If yes, give yourself a gold star. The Lost World of Imagination is in your sights. Your stories will get written.

Is everyone better than me?

This thought is guaranteed to give you writer's block, so show it the bullwhip, too. How good a writer you become is up to you and how hard you work at it. Only *you* can tell your stories, and if you don't succeed as a fiction writer, you might become a top journalist or a successful advertising writer.

Now it's your turn

Prove it

Right now, prove to yourself that you can write. Watch your favorite TV or film adventure. Rewrite your own version of the story. Change the characters or turn a minor character into the hero. Taking notes on how well TV stories work can teach you a lot about constructing a gripping narrative.

The loneliness of being a writer can often stop people from writing. So if you start feeling marooned, call in some friends to try out your story ideas on.

Try out operation think tank

Sit in a circle and tell your friends your story so far. Put on the skin of your hero and let your friends interrogate you. Who are you? What do you really want? What is at stake? What or who is stopping you from solving your problems? What can you do about this? They could ask you about your history, too—where you came from or how you got lost.

Build a character

Group brainstorming can help bring your character to life. Start by writing a brief character description at the top of a sheet of paper. After two minutes, pass it to a friend to add his or her ideas. When two minutes are up, the next person develops the description. Mull over the results. Have you learned anything new about your character?

GETTING STARTED · SETTING THE SCENE · CHARACTERS · VIEWPOINT

Use the three-card trick

Make a group story. First cut up some scrap paper into 36 squares. Choose someone to do the writing. Then go around the circle and brainstorm 12 ideas for new characters—perhaps include a big-game hunter. Next brainstorm 12 objects—maybe start with a treasure chest. Finally, brainstorm 12 interesting locations—such as the Great Wall of China. Shuffle the three piles and place them face down in the middle. Everyone should choose one card and take turns to weave the character, place, or object into a story. The end result will be something like a chapter synopsis.

TIPS AND TECHNIQUES

When you are stuck for words, go for a walk to inspire ideas. Or try looking under your bed. Everything you threw there months ago will have a memory attached to it. Perhaps it's just the clue you need to restart your story. Sometimes a stalled story simply needs to brew for a while. Start something new while you wait.

Pick and mix

Everyone chooses a sentence from his or her favorite adventure story. All the choices must be worked into a group story.

Keep a diary

Many adventure stories are written as diary entries, so keeping your own diary is useful. It also helps prevent writer's block. Set yourself a daily target, say 300 words. See how you can turn the day's events into an anecdote or dramatic story. Definitely record all holiday travels.

TAKE THE NEXT STEP

Well done! Finishing your first story is a great achievement. You have reached the Lost World of Imagination and created something entirely new. You have proved you can write and probably learned a lot about yourself, too. But now it's time to set out on a new adventure and start a new story.

Write another story

Perhaps while you were writing the first story, some new ideas cropped up and you made a note of them in your "ideas file." Take them out. Do they still excite you? If so, go back to the start of this book and repeat some of the brainstorming exercises to help you develop the ideas further. This time, you already know you can write a story.

Consider a sequel to your first story

When thinking about your next work, ask yourself: Do I want to send the characters I created in my first story on another adventure? Is there more to tell about them in a sequel? Occasionally, adventure stories are written as trilogies, like *Lionboy*, by Zizou Corder. The three-book structure mimics the beginning, middle, and end of all stories. Book one starts the adventure. Book two deepens and complicates the story. Book three brings the story to a climax and a satisfying conclusion.

Now it's your turn

Become the hero

To see if your hero is ready for a new adventure, try this exercise. Take a large sheet of paper, and at the center draw your main character inside a circle. Then draw six lines radiating out to six more circles. Now imagine you are the hero looking around for a new challenge. Ask yourself: What is my new problem? Where am I going next? For 10 minutes, brainstorm your first thoughts, putting one idea in each of the circles. If some of your results seem totally crazy, don't worry. You may find that, with a little more thought, they are good ideas after all.

Make old characters reappear

Sometimes a hero is so intriguing and pushy that they demand more tales about them. Joan Aiken's Dido Twite is just such a character. This brave, smart-talking, smart-thinking waif first appeared in *Black Hearts in Battersea* (a sequel to *The Wolves of Willoughby Chase*), only to be lost at sea at the end of the book. But in *Nightbirds on Nantucket,* she comes sailing back aboard Captain Coffin's whaler and is soon set to foil another wicked plot.

You can learn a lot by reading about famous writers' own writing adventures. Most will tell you that it took a long time before their stories were published. They will also say that it is often hard to earn a living as a writer. Here is some advice from other writers.

David Almond

David Almond (author of *Kit's Wilderness*) had always wanted to be a writer. As a child, he loved his local library and imagined his own books on the shelves. But it wasn't until he was much older and had been teaching for some years that he began to write.

Almond says, "Give your story a title from the very start, even if you know you'll change it. The title will help the story take on a life of its own."

He adds, "Believe that you are becoming a good writer. Train yourself to find the good bits and to throw out or change the bad."

Margaret Mahy

Margaret Mahy (author of *24 Hours*) sets her stories in her New Zealand homeland. She started writing when she was 7, but she was 33 and working as a librarian before she published her first stories. She knows it is rare for writers to have success with their first book. They all spend a lot of time working really hard and having their work rejected by publishers before they are published.

Mahy says, "Know within yourself why certain books work well for you."

Sharon Creech

Sharon Creech based her first young people's book, *Absolutely Normal Chaos*, on her own noisy family life in South Euclid, Ohio She even used her brothers' real names in the book. She used to teach literature and says that reading and talking about great books helped her to understand how to craft interesting stories.

Lois Lowry

"Read a lot," says Lois Lowry (right), author of *Messenger* and many other books for young readers. "I mean really a LOT. And when you're reading, think about how the author did things."

Michael Morpurgo

Michael Morpurgo (author of *Kensuke's Kingdom*) used to be a teacher, but now he writes and runs a charity called Farms for City Children Project. He lives on a farm, and when he has trouble writing, he walks around the fields telling himself the story out loud. He does a lot of research for each book and a lot of dreaming. Then he writes up to six versions. He doesn't usually know how his story will end when he starts, but he leaves it to his characters to sort out.

He says, "Write from the heart—as you feel your story, as you see it."

When your first story has been resting in your desk drawer for a month, take it out and do some revision. You will be able to read it with fresh eyes, and it will be easier to spot any flaws.

Edit your work

Reading your work aloud will help you to simplify rambling sentences and correct dialogue that doesn't flow. Cut out all unnecessary adjectives and adverbs, and extra words like "very" and "really." This will instantly make your writing crisper. Once you have cut down the number of words, decide how well the story works. Does it have a satisfying end? Has your hero resolved the conflict in the best possible way? When your story is as good as can be, write it out again or type it up on a computer. This is your manuscript.

Think of a title

It is important to think of a good title—something intriguing and eye-catching. Think about some titles you know and like.

Be professional

If you have a computer, you can type up your manuscript and give it a professional presentation. Manuscripts should always be printed on one side of white paper, with wide margins and double spacing. Pages should be numbered, and new chapters should start on a new page. You can also include your title as a header on the top of each page. At the front, you should have a title page with your name, address, telephone number, and e-mail address on it. Repeat this information on the last page.

Make your own book

If your school has its own computer lab, why not use it to publish your own story or to make a story anthology (collection) with your friends. A computer will let you choose your own font (print style) or justify the text (making even margins like a professionally printed page). When you have typed and saved your story to a file, you can edit it quickly with the spelling and grammar checker, or move sections of your story around using the cut-and-paste tool, which saves a lot of rewriting.

Having your story on a computer file also means you can print a copy whenever you need one, or revise the whole story if you want to.

Design a cover

Once your story is in good shape, you can print it out and use the computer to design the cover. A graphics program will let you scan and print your own artwork, or download ready-made graphics. Or you could use your own digital photographs and learn how to manipulate them on-screen to produce some highly original images. You can use yourself or friends as models for your story's heroes.

TIPS AND TECHNIQUES

Whether you write your story on a computer or by hand, always make a copy before you give it to others to read. Otherwise, if they lose it, you will have lost all your precious work.

REACH YOUR AUDIENCE

The next step is to find an audience for your piece of adventure fiction. Family members or classmates may be receptive. Or you may want to share your work via a Web site, a literary magazine, or publishing house.

Some places to publish your story

There are several magazines and a number of writing Web sites that accept stories and novel chapters from young adventure-fiction writers. Some give writing advice. Several run regular competitions. Each site has its own rules about submitting work to them, so make sure you read them carefully before you send in a story. Here are some more ideas:

- Send stories to your school newspaper.
  If your school doesn't have a newspaper, start your own with like-minded friends.

- Keep your eyes peeled when reading your local newspaper or magazines. They might be running a writing competition you could enter.

- Check with local museums and colleges. Some run creative-writing workshops during school holidays.

Start a writing club

Starting a writing club or workshop group and exchanging stories is a great way of getting your fiction story out there. It will also get you used to criticism from others, which will prove invaluable in learning how to write. Your local library might be kind enough to provide a space for such a club.

Finding a book publisher

Study the market and find out which publishers are most likely to publish adventure fiction. Addresses of publishers and information about whether they accept submissions can be found in writers' handbooks at your local library. Bear in mind that manuscripts that haven't been asked for or paid for by a publisher—unsolicited submissions—are rarely published. Secure any submission with a staple or paperclip and always enclose a short letter (explaining what you have sent) and a stamped, self-addressed envelope for the story's return.

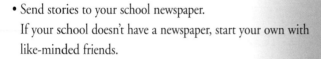

GETTING STARTED | SETTING THE SCENE | CHARACTERS | VIEWPOINT

Don't give up

If your story is rejected by an editor, don't despair. See it as a chance to make the story better and try again. Remember, having your work published is wonderful, but it is not the only thing. Being able to make up stories is a gift, so why not give yours to someone you love? Read it to a younger brother or sister. Tell it to your grandfather. Find your audience.

Some final words

Becoming a writer is the biggest adventure of all. Every story you write will change you in some way. You will feel you have been on a special journey. Even better, there is no limit to where you might go next. So keep on trekking to those new horizons.

READ! WRITE!

Head for the next big adventure!

Case study

David Almond spent five years writing an adult novel that was rejected by many publishers. Then he had the idea of a filthy, irritable, arthritic man living off live spiders in a rundown garage, and he began the story of the mysterious winged being, Skellig. It became a major best seller. Almond is proof that good writers sometimes try too hard to write for the wrong audience.

GLOSSARY

back story—the history of characters and events that happened before the story begins

chapter synopsis—an outline that describes briefly what happens in each chapter

cliffhanger—ending a chapter or scene of a story at a nail-biting moment

dramatic irony—when the reader knows something the characters don't

editing—removing all unnecessary words from your story, correcting errors, and rewriting the text until the story is the best it can be

editor—the person at a publishing house who finds new books to publish and advises authors on how to improve their stories by telling them what needs to be added or cut

first-person viewpoint—a viewpoint that allows a single character to tell the story as if he or she had written it; readers feel as if that character is talking directly to them; for example: "It was July when I left for Timbuktu. Just the thought of going back there made my heart sing."

foreshadowing—dropping hints of coming events or dangers that are essential to the outcome of the story

genre—a particular type of fiction, such as fantasy, historical, adventure, or science fiction

internal critic—the voice in your mind that constantly picks holes in your work and makes you want to give up

manuscript—your story when it is written down, either typed or by hand

metaphor—calling a man "a mouse" is a metaphor, a word picture; from it we learn in one word that the man is timid or weak, not that he is actually a mouse

narrative—the telling of a story

omniscient viewpoint—an all-seeing narrator that sees all the characters and tells readers how they are acting and feeling

plot—the sequence of events that drive a story forward; the problems that the hero must resolve

point of view (POV)—the eyes through which a story is told

publisher—a person or company who pays for an author's manuscript to be printed as a book and who distributes and sells that book

sequel—a story that carries an existing one forward

simile—saying something is like something else, a word picture, such as "clouds like frayed lace"

synopsis—a short summary that describes what a story is about and introduces the main characters

theme—the main idea behind your story, such as overcoming a weakness, the importance of friendship, or good versus evil. A story can have more than one theme.

third-person viewpoint—a viewpoint that describes the events of the story through a single character's eyes, such as "Jem's heart leapt in his throat. He'd been dreading this moment for months."

unsolicited submission—a manuscript that is sent to a publisher without being requested; these submissions usually end up in the "slush pile," where they may wait a long time to be read

writer's block—when writers think they can no longer write or have used up all their ideas

FURTHER INFORMATION

Visit your local libraries and make friends with the librarians. They can direct you to useful sources of information, including magazines that publish young people's short fiction. You can learn your craft and read great stories at the same time. Librarians will also know if any published authors are scheduled to speak in your area.

Many authors visit schools and offer writing workshops. Ask your teacher to invite a favorite author to speak at your school.

On the Web

For more information on this topic, use FactHound.
1. Go to *www.facthound.com*
2. Type in this book or this book ID: 0756516382
3. Click on the *Fetch It* button.
FactHound will find the best Web sites for you.

Read more adventure stories

Alexander, Lloyd. *The Rope Trick.* New York: Dutton Children's Books, 2002.

Anderson, Janet S. *Going Through the Gate.* New York: Dutton Children's Books, 1997.

Buck, Pearl S. *The Big Wave.* New York: J. Day Co., 1973.

Collins, Suzanne. *Gregor the Overlander.* New York: Scholastic Press, 2003.

Corder, Zizou. *Lionboy.* New York: Dial Books, 2004.

Cooper, Susan. *King of Shadows.* New York: Margaret K. McElderry Books, 1999.

Funke, Cornelia. *The Thief Lord.* New York: Scholastic, 2002.

Gleitzman, Morris. *Two Weeks with the Queen.* New York: Putnam, 1991.

Horowitz, Anthony. *Stormbreaker.* New York: Philomel Books, 2001.

Ibbotson, Eva. *The Secret of Platform 13.* New York: Dutton Children's Books, 1998.

London, Jack. *White Fang.* West Berlin, N.J.: Townsend Press, 2003.

McCaughrean, Geraldine. *The Kite Rider.* New York: HarperCollins, 2002.

Naylor, Phyllis Reynolds. *The Fear Place.* New York: Atheneum Books for Young Readers, 1994.

Paulsen, Gary. *Hatchet.* New York: Aladdin Paperbacks, 1999.

Rees, Celia. *Pirates!* New York: Bloomsbury, 2003.

Roberts, Willo Davis. *Hostage.* New York: Atheneum Books for Young Readers, 2000.

Taylor, Theodore. *Ice Drift.* Orlando, Fla.: Harcourt, 2004.

Read all the Write Your Own books:

Write Your Own Adventure Story
ISBN: 0-7565-1638-2

Write Your Own Fantasy Story
ISBN: 0-7565-1639-0

Write Your Own Historical Fiction Story
ISBN: 0-7565-1640-4

Write Your Own Mystery Story
ISBN: 0-7565-1641-2

Write Your Own Realistic Fiction Story
ISBN: 0-7565-1642-0

Write Your Own Science Fiction Story
ISBN: 0-7565-1643-9

INDEX

Picture Credits: Alamy: 14-15 all. Bridgeman Art Library: 13t, 24 all, 35tr, 36-37c, 38-39c. Corbis RF: 3, 4-5 all, 22b, 27 all, 28t, 29b, 34 all, 35b, 39r, 40l, 40-41b, 42-43b, 43t, 44-45 all, 46-47 all, 52-53c, 54t, 56-57 all. Creatas: 6-7 all, 8-9 all, 13b, 16-17 all, 18-19b, 19c, 22-23c, 37tr, 48t, 49t, 50t, 50-51c, 51r, 52t. FLPA: 10l, 18t, 19t, 20-21 all, 26-27c, 28l, 29c, 30b, 50-51b, 52b. Fotosearch: 28t, 58-59 all. Rex Features: 10t, 10-11c, 11r, 12, 22t, 25 all, 26t, 28-29c, 32-33 all, 42t, 48-49b, 54b, 55 all, 60-61c.